OUTSOURCING SECRETS

Unlock the Power of Outsourcing to
Skyrocket Your Online Business

Ray Goodwin

CONTENTS

LIABILITY DISCLAIMER

The information contained within this book is intended for informational purposes only and should not be construed as legal or professional advice. The authors and publishers of this book are not responsible for any losses or damages that may arise from the use of the information contained within.

The reader assumes full responsibility for any decisions made based on the information in this book. The authors and publishers do not endorse any particular method, service or product mentioned in this book and are not responsible for any consequences resulting from their use.

The reader should exercise caution and discretion when making life changing decisions, and should be aware of the risks and potential consequences of their actions. This book is not a substitute for professional or legal advice and should not be relied upon as such.

By reading and using the information in this book, the reader acknowledges and agrees to hold harmless the authors, publishers, and any other parties involved in the creation or distribution of this book from any and all liability, claims, damages, or losses that may arise from their use of the information contained herein.

CHAPTER 1: INTRODUCTION TO OUTSOURCING

Welcome to Outsourcing Secrets, a practical guide to taking your online business to the next level. As an experienced online entrepreneur with many years in the industry, I can tell you that outsourcing is one of the most important strategies for growing your business and maximizing profits.

Outsourcing is all about delegating tasks and responsibilities to other people or companies who specialize in those areas, allowing you to focus on what you do best. Whether you're a solopreneur or running a larger company, outsourcing can help you save time, reduce costs, and increase productivity.

In this book, I'll be sharing my personal experiences and insights into outsourcing for online businesses. We'll cover everything from finding the right freelancers and contractors to managing projects effectively and communicating with remote teams.

We'll explore real-world examples of successful outsourcing strategies, discuss common pitfalls and challenges, and provide actionable advice on how to overcome them.

Whether you're just starting out or looking for ways to scale your existing business, Outsourcing Secrets has something for everyone.

Let's Begin

Outsourcing has gained tremendous importance and acceptance over the last few decades. It has significantly altered the way businesses operate and has become a crucial part of today's global economy. But, before we delve deeper into the various facets of outsourcing, let's begin by defining what outsourcing exactly is.

Definition of Outsourcing

Outsourcing refers to the practice of hiring an external company or service provider to perform tasks or services typically done in-house. In the outsourcing model, a company contracts specific business processes or services to a third-party vendor, who then takes responsibility for performing the task efficiently and cost-effectively.

Outsourcing has enabled companies to leverage the expertise and specialization of other firms and access resources that are not readily available within their own organizations. By outsourcing, companies can focus on their core competencies while delegating non-core functions to specialized third-party service providers.

History of Outsourcing

Outsourcing is not a new concept and has been practiced in various forms throughout history. In the 18th century, the East India Company hired local laborers to produce textile goods in India for export to the British market. During the 19th century, companies in the United States often outsourced work to cottage industries and small workshops, enabling them to reduce costs and increase productivity.

The modern form of outsourcing, however, can be traced back to the 1960s, when large corporations began to delegate certain functions such as janitorial and security services to other specialist companies. Since then, outsourcing has grown exponentially, driven by technological advancements and increased global competition.

Types of Outsourcing

Outsourcing can be divided into three distinct categories, each with its own unique characteristics and advantages:

1. Information Technology Outsourcing (ITO):

ITO involves outsourcing of information technology services such as software development, technical support, and data center management.

2. Business Process Outsourcing (BPO):

BPO involves outsourcing of non-core business processes such as human resources, finance and accounting, and customer service.

3. Knowledge Process Outsourcing (KPO):

KPO involves outsourcing of complex business processes such as research and development, analytics, and technical writing.

Advantages of Outsourcing

Outsourcing offers several advantages to companies that go beyond just cost savings. Some of these advantages are:

> ➤ Increased efficiency - Outsourcing enables companies to focus on their core competencies and delegate non-core functions to specialist service providers, leading to increased efficiency.

> ➤ Access to specialized skills and expertise - Outsourcing allows companies to tap into the specialized skills and

expertise of external vendors that may not be available within their own organization.

➢ Reduced costs - Outsourcing can significantly reduce fixed and variable costs associated with non-core functions.

➢ Scalability - Outsourcing vendors can provide services and support that are scalable according to the needs of the organization, enabling businesses to grow without any major disruptions.

➢ Flexibility - Outsourcing can provide much-needed flexibility in resource management, allowing companies to manage ebbs and flows in workloads.

Disadvantages of Outsourcing

Along with advantages, outsourcing also has some disadvantages that companies need to consider:

➢ Loss of control - Outsourcing requires relinquishing control over certain business processes, which can result in reduced transparency and flexibility.

➢ Communication challenges - Overcoming language and cultural differences can prove to be challenging, leading to communication issues and substandard results.

➢ Quality risks - Outsourcing can result in quality risks if the service provider does not meet expectations or fails to deliver as promised.

➢ Security risks - Outsourcing sensitive business processes can lead to data security and privacy risks if not handled appropriately.

➢ Cultural disconnects - Outsourcing to different countries may result in cultural misunderstandings that can impact the quality of work and overall relationship.

Common misconceptions about Outsourcing

Outsourcing is often misunderstood and associated with negative connotations. Some common misconceptions about outsourcing include:

- ❖ Outsourcing always results in job losses - While outsourcing does result in job losses in some cases, it can also create new jobs.

- ❖ Outsourcing always results in lower quality - Outsourcing can lead to lower quality work, but only if the service provider is not adequately vetted, or if communication channels are not established properly.

- ❖ Outsourcing is always done to cut costs - While cost reduction is a significant factor in outsourcing, it is not the only reason companies opt for it. Outsourcing can lead to access to specialized skills, increased efficiency and expertise.

Factors to consider before outsourcing

Before outsourcing, companies need to assess various factors to ensure that it is the right decision for their business. Some key factors to consider are:

- ❖ Cost-benefit analysis - Assessing the costs and benefits of outsourcing is critical to ensure that it aligns with the overall strategy of the organization.

- ❖ Vendor selection - Properly vetting and selecting the right outsourcing partner is crucial to the success of the outsourcing relationship.

- ❖ Quality control - Ensuring that service quality complies with industry standards and benchmarks is crucial.

- ❖ Communication channels - Establishing clear

communication channels and protocols to enable collaboration and information sharing is essential.

❖ Data security - Ensuring that service providers comply with data security and privacy policies is critical to protect confidential information.

❖ Legal compliance - Ensuring that outsourcing relationships meet and comply with local laws and regulations is essential.

Importance of outsourcing in today's economy

Outsourcing has become a fundamental part of today's global economy, and it plays a vital role in enabling businesses to compete at a global level. It has helped to reshape industries and business models, and it has enabled companies to access specialized skills, expertise, and resources to improve their performance, productivity, and efficiency.

Outsourcing is not only limited to large corporations, as small and medium-sized businesses can also leverage outsourcing to grow their businesses and remain competitive. Outsourcing has grown rapidly over the past few decades and will continue to be a significant part of the business landscape moving forward.

In the next chapter, we will discuss how to find the right outsourcing partner and the essential steps that companies need to follow to ensure successful outsourcing relationships.

CHAPTER 2: FINDING THE RIGHT OUTSOURCING PARTNER

Outsourcing has become a popular business practice, and many companies have already experienced the benefits it offers. However, finding the right outsourcing partner can be challenging. Choosing the wrong outsourcing partner can lead to possible business failure, so it is crucial to invest time and effort in identifying and evaluating potential outsourcing partners. In this chapter, we will discuss the steps you need to take to find and evaluate the right outsourcing partner for your business needs.

Identifying Your Outsourcing Needs

Before you start looking for potential outsourcing partners, you must first identify your outsourcing needs. List down the processes or tasks that you want to outsource. It would be best to consider outsourcing functions that could significantly benefit your business and improve its operations.

For example, if you own a marketing agency, you might want to outsource web design or copywriting. This could free up time for your in-house team to focus on marketing, strategy, and creative development.

Researching Potential Outsourcing Partners

After you have identified your outsourcing needs, the next step is to research potential outsourcing partners. Search online to find companies that offer the services you require. Make sure to read their website, case studies, and testimonials. Check out their social media profiles and look for reviews in business directories.

You could also request recommendations from colleagues in your industry or other business owners in your network. Many people are often happy to share their outsourcing experiences.

Evaluating Outsourcing Partners

Once you have identified potential outsourcing partners, the next step is to evaluate them. Conduct a thorough evaluation to ensure that you choose the right outsourcing partner. You can evaluate outsourcing partners based on the following criteria:

❖ Expertise: Choose an outsourcing partner that has the necessary experience and knowledge of the processes you want to outsource.

❖ Reputation: Look for an outsourcing partner with a positive reputation in the industry. Check for online reviews and ask for references.

❖ Communication: Choose an outsourcing partner that has clear communication channels and can communicate effectively with you and your team.

❖ Flexibility: Choose an outsourcing partner that is flexible and willing to adapt to your business needs.

❖ Price: Compare prices and ensure that you choose an outsourcing partner that offers competitive pricing.

Assessing Language and Cultural Barriers

When outsourcing, language barriers can occur between you and your outsourcing partner. This can lead to miscommunication, misunderstandings, and inaccurate output. Cultural differences can also be a significant obstacle to effective outsourcing partnerships, so it's important to assess your potential outsourcing partner's cultural affinities.

Ask potential outsourcing partners about their language proficiency and consider their cultural background. Ensure that they have experience working with clients with similar cultural backgrounds to yours.

Determining Clear Communication Channels

It's important to establish clear communication channels from the beginning of your outsourcing partnership. This is essential for communicating expectations, getting progress updates, and addressing possible concerns. Determine the communication channels that will be used, including phone calls, email, video conferences, and project management tools.

Creating an Outsourcing Contract

Once you have established clear communication channels and have identified the right outsourcing partner, it's time to create an outsourcing contract. The outsourcing contract should lay out the terms and conditions of the outsourcing partnership. It should include the scope of work, responsibilities of both parties, completion schedules, and the pricing structure.

Set Expectations and Goals

Setting expectations and goals is an essential element of any outsourcing partnership. Discuss with your outsourcing partner the specific tasks, deadlines, and metrics that they need to deliver. Ensure that they understand your objectives and goals, and that they are all aligned with your company's mission and vision. The outsourcing partner should be aware of your expected quality standards and communication protocols, as well as any possible cultural or language differences.

Creating a Mutually Beneficial Relationship

A mutually beneficial relationship with your outsourcing partner can lead to a long-term partnership that benefits both parties. Establish a good working relationship that fosters trust and transparency. Be open and honest about issues and concerns and encourage your outsourcing partners to do the same. This way, you can address challenges and find mutually beneficial solutions.

Conclusion

Finding the right outsourcing partner is a crucial step in outsourcing. It requires time and effort to research potential partners, evaluate their expertise, and assess their language and cultural barriers. Determining clear communication channels is essential for the success of any outsourcing partnership. Creating an outsourcing contract, setting expectations and goals, and establishing a mutually beneficial relationship can lead to long-term success for your business. Remember that outsourcing is not a one-size-fits-all solution, and you should choose the outsourcing partner that suits your specific needs.

CHAPTER 3: MANAGING OUTSOURCING RELATIONSHIPS

Outsourcing is not just about finding the right partner, it's about building a long-term relationship that is based on mutual understanding, clear communication, trust, and accountability. In this chapter, we will explore the key elements of managing outsourcing relationships, including defining roles and responsibilities, establishing lines of communication, maintaining trust with your outsourcing partner, keeping track of progress and results, monitoring performance and quality, addressing issues and concerns, managing cultural differences, and building a long-term relationship.

Defining roles and responsibilities

One of the first steps in managing outsourcing relationships is to define the roles and responsibilities for both parties. This includes identifying what tasks and functions will be outsourced, who will be in charge of managing the relationship, and what the deliverables and timelines are. Defining roles and responsibilities upfront can help avoid misunderstandings or conflicts later on. It's important to have a clear understanding of expectations and deliverables from both parties to ensure alignment and that the desired outcomes are achieved.

Establishing lines of communication

Clear communication is a critical component of effective outsourcing relationships. It's important to establish lines of communication early on and to define who the key points of contact are for each party. This includes identifying the channels of communication such as email or a dedicated chat platform and agreeing on response times. By having clear communication with your outsourcing partner, you will be able to address any issues or concerns in a timely manner, which can help avoid delays or misunderstandings.

Maintaining trust with your outsourcing partner

Trust is a key ingredient in successful outsourcing relationships. By maintaining a level of trust with your outsourcing partner, you can ensure that they will meet their commitments, deliver high-quality work, and handle sensitive information with care. Building trust takes time, but it starts with transparency and clear communication. It's important to keep your outsourcing partner informed of any changes or updates that may impact the project or the relationship, and to address any issues or concerns promptly and professionally.

Keeping track of progress and results

It's important to keep track of progress and results throughout the outsourcing relationship. This includes tracking deliverables, timelines, and costs, and reporting on progress regularly. By tracking progress and results, you can identify any issues or concerns early on, and address them before they become bigger problems. You can also evaluate the return on investment (ROI) of the outsourcing relationship and make adjustments as needed to ensure that you are getting the desired results.

Monitoring performance and quality

Monitoring performance and quality is a critical element of managing outsourcing relationships. This includes conducting regular quality checks, evaluating the performance of individual team members, and addressing any issues or concerns promptly. By monitoring performance and quality, you can ensure that your outsourcing partner is meeting the expected standards and that the project is on track. You can also provide feedback and support to help your outsourcing partner improve their performance and deliver better results.

Addressing issues and concerns

Issues and concerns may arise during the outsourcing relationship, and it's important to address them promptly and professionally. This includes identifying the root cause of the issue, developing a plan to resolve it, and implementing the plan effectively. By addressing issues and concerns effectively, you can maintain trust and credibility with your outsourcing partner and ensure that the project stays on track.

Managing cultural differences

Cultural differences can pose challenges in outsourcing relationships. It's important to be aware of cultural differences and to manage them effectively. This includes understanding the cultural norms and expectations of your outsourcing partner, being open to different perspectives and ways of doing things and adapting to cultural differences as needed. By managing cultural differences effectively, you can build stronger relationships with your outsourcing partner, and ensure that the project is successful.

Building a long-term relationship

Building a long-term relationship is the ultimate goal of outsourcing. By building a long-term relationship, you can ensure continuity in your outsourcing arrangements, maintain a level of trust and understanding, and leverage the knowledge and expertise of your outsourcing partner. Building a long-term relationship takes time, but it starts with a commitment to open communication, transparency, and mutual respect. By investing in the relationship, you can reap the rewards of successful outsourcing over the long-term.

In conclusion, managing outsourcing relationships is critical to the success of any outsourcing initiative. By defining roles and responsibilities, establishing lines of communication, maintaining trust with your outsourcing partner, keeping track of progress and results, monitoring performance and quality, addressing issues and concerns, managing cultural differences, and building a long-term relationship, you can ensure that your outsourcing arrangements are successful and achieve the desired results.

CHAPTER 4: THE PROS AND CONS OF OFFSHORE OUTSOURCING

Offshore outsourcing is a business practice that has been gaining popularity over the last several years. It involves hiring an external company, typically located in another country, to complete tasks or provide services that would otherwise be performed in-house. The rise of technology and globalization has made offshore outsourcing increasingly common. In this chapter, we will explore the pros and cons of offshore outsourcing.

Definition of Offshore Outsourcing

Offshore outsourcing is outsourcing to a company in a foreign country. For example, a company based in the United States may choose to offshore outsource its customer service operations to a company in India. Offshore outsourcing is sometimes referred to as international outsourcing or offshoring.

Advantages of Offshore Outsourcing

The primary advantage of offshore outsourcing is cost savings. Companies can often find lower-cost labor and resources in other countries. This can allow them to save money on wages, benefits, and infrastructure costs.

Another advantage of offshore outsourcing is access to a larger talent pool. Companies can tap into a wider range of skills and experience by outsourcing to companies in other countries. This can be particularly valuable for specialized tasks that require niche expertise.

Offshore outsourcing can also provide companies with more flexibility in managing their workforce. By outsourcing certain functions, companies can expand or contract their workforce as needed. This can be particularly useful for businesses with cyclical or seasonal demand.

Disadvantages of Offshore Outsourcing

One of the main disadvantages of offshore outsourcing is the potential for language and cultural barriers. Communication can be challenging when working with individuals from different backgrounds. Differences in time zones can also create scheduling difficulties.

Offshore outsourcing can also lead to quality control issues. Companies may struggle to monitor and manage the work being done by external partners. This can result in lower quality work, missed deadlines, or other problems.

Another potential drawback of offshore outsourcing is the risk to data security and privacy. Companies that outsource tasks involving sensitive data or intellectual property run the risk of that information being compromised. It is critical to ensure that the offshore outsourcing partner has adequate security measures in place.

Common Myths about Offshore Outsourcing

There are a number of common myths about offshore outsourcing that can lead businesses astray. Perhaps the most persistent myth is that offshore outsourcing is always cheaper than using domestic resources. While it is true that offshore outsourcing can provide cost savings, there are many factors that can impact the cost competitiveness of different approaches.

Another myth is that offshore outsourcing always leads to a loss of domestic jobs. While it is true that some jobs may be outsourced overseas, other jobs may be created in support of the outsourcing initiative. Additionally, outsourcing certain functions may allow domestic workers to focus on higher value work that cannot be outsourced.

Choosing the Right Offshore Outsourcing Destination

Choosing the right offshore outsourcing destination is critical to the success of the initiative. There are many factors to consider in making this decision, including language and cultural compatibility, infrastructure quality, political stability, workforce skills, and legal considerations.

India has long been a popular destination for offshore outsourcing, due in part to its large workforce, diverse range of skills, and English language proficiency. Other popular destinations include China, the Philippines, and Eastern Europe.

Managing Language and Cultural Differences

Language and cultural differences can pose challenges to offshore outsourcing relationships. Companies can take a number of steps to manage these challenges, including using translation services, establishing clear communication channels, and providing cultural training to employees.

Managing Time Zone Differences

Managing time zone differences can be another challenge of offshore outsourcing. This can be addressed by establishing clear communication protocols and scheduling regular check-ins at a mutually-convenient time. This may require some flexibility on the part of both parties.

Ensuring Data Security and Privacy

Ensuring data security and privacy is critical when outsourcing tasks that involve sensitive data or intellectual property. Companies should carefully vet offshore outsourcing partners to ensure that they have adequate security measures in place. They may also want to consider using secure communication channels and establishing data access controls.

Conclusion

Offshore outsourcing can provide significant benefits to companies, including cost savings, access to specialized skills, and more flexible workforce management. However, there are also a number of risks and challenges associated with offshore outsourcing. Companies must carefully weigh the pros and cons and choose the right offshore outsourcing partner to ensure success. By effectively managing language and cultural differences, time zone differences, and data security and privacy concerns, companies can reap the rewards of offshore outsourcing while minimizing the risks.

CHAPTER 5: THE COST OF OUTSOURCING

Outsourcing can help businesses save money while providing additional benefits such as gaining access to top talent, reducing operational costs, and increasing efficiency. However, it's important for businesses to understand the different cost factors involved in outsourcing to properly assess its impact on their bottom line.

There are several cost-saving opportunities that businesses can take advantage of, but outsourcing does not always result in cost savings. It's essential to analyze the ROI of outsourcing before taking the plunge.

Understanding the different cost factors involved in outsourcing

When outsourcing, businesses should consider the following cost factors:

❖ Labor cost: One of the most significant cost factors to consider is labor costs. Businesses can substantially save money by outsourcing tasks to countries where labor is cheaper.

❖ Legal and compliance costs: Outsourcing to offshore locations may come with additional legal and compliance costs such as data privacy, intellectual property rights, and local laws. In addition, businesses may need to invest in a legal team to ensure compliance.

❖ Communication costs: Communication is critical in outsourcing. Businesses should consider costs such as telecom expenses, IT infrastructure, or hiring translators as part of their outsourcing strategy.

❖ Traveling costs: In instances where traveling is necessary, businesses should account for visa fees, airfare, accommodation, and other expenses that may arise.

Comparing the costs of outsourcing to in-house production

When comparing costs, businesses should consider both direct and indirect expenses. Direct expenses include salaries, benefits, taxes, equipment, and supplies. Indirect expenses include rent, utilities, insurance, training, recruitment, and management.

Outsourcing can help businesses save money on overhead costs, as the outsourced team is typically responsible for its own expenses. For example, rent, utilities, equipment, and supplies are typically provided by the service provider. Outsourcing can let businesses allocate internal resources towards other higher-priority projects.

Assessing the impact of outsourcing on your company's bottom line

Cost savings are not the only benefits of outsourcing. In some cases, businesses may wish to prioritize quality or time to market over cost savings. Outsourcing to an offshore location can save significantly on labor costs but may require a language barrier and potentially lower quality output.

Analyzing the ROI of outsourcing

Utilizing the ROI of outsourcing allows businesses to evaluate the success of their outsourcing initiatives. ROI measures the overall profitability of outsourcing and is calculated by subtracting outsourcing expenses from savings while incorporating revenue generated from the outsourcing arrangement. This analysis can also uncover areas where outsourcing is not benefiting the business and potential ways to mitigate financial risks.

Budgeting for outsourcing

Understanding the costs of outsourcing tasks should be factored into your budget. Having a clear understanding of the costs involved in outsourcing allows businesses to allocate resources accordingly. Additionally, it provides businesses with transparency of the potential cost savings that an outsourced team can offer.

Negotiating pricing and contracts with your outsourcing partners

To secure the best possible deal when outsourcing, businesses should negotiate pricing and contracts with their potential outsourcing partners. Negotiating terms and contracts can result in long-term cost savings and produce positive outcomes for both parties.

Mitigating financial risks associated with outsourcing

When outsourcing, businesses must take steps to mitigate financial risks. Businesses should have a contingency plan or start small to reduce the risk of a complete failure in outsourcing.

Identifying cost-saving opportunities through outsourcing

Apart from labor cost savings, businesses can find other cost-saving opportunities through outsourcing. For example, outsourcing can assist in the automation of processes and reduce overhead expenses, which can increase efficiency and decrease the workload for the outsourced team while lowering overall costs.

In conclusion, outsourcing offers businesses an opportunity to cut costs and create a stronger, more efficient company. However, it's important to be aware of and understand the various cost factors associated with outsourcing. Before outsourcing, businesses need to assess both the direct and indirect costs, compare outsourcing costs with in-house production, analyze the ROI of outsourcing, and negotiate contracts and pricing. Understanding the cost-saving opportunities presented by outsourcing can help businesses develop a cost-effective strategy while effectively mitigating financial risk.

CHAPTER 6: RECRUITING AND MANAGING A REMOTE TEAM

In today's digital age, having a remote team is becoming increasingly popular among businesses of all sizes. A remote team allows businesses to access a diverse talent pool and take advantage of flexible working arrangements. However, managing a remote team can prove to be challenging, especially if the team is spread out across different time zones and cultures. In this chapter, we will explore the benefits of having a remote team, the challenges that come with managing a remote team, and how to find and recruit talented remote workers.

Benefits of having a remote team

One of the most significant benefits of having a remote team is access to a wider talent pool. When businesses limit themselves to hiring locally, they miss out on a great deal of talent that may be located outside their immediate area. With a remote team, businesses can recruit from anywhere in the world, meaning they can find the best fit for their team and access a range of skills and experience.

Having a remote team also allows for greater flexibility

in working arrangements. Remote workers can work from anywhere, meaning they can work at times that suit them best. This flexibility can lead to increased productivity and greater satisfaction among employees.

Challenges of managing a remote team

While having a remote team has many benefits, managing a remote team also presents unique challenges. One of the most significant challenges is keeping everyone on the same page. With a remote team, communication can be more difficult, and it can be harder to ensure that everyone is working towards the same goals.

Another challenge is ensuring that remote workers are productive and accountable. Without face-to-face supervision, it can be challenging to monitor the progress of remote workers, and they may feel isolated or disconnected from their team.

Finding and recruiting remote workers

Finding and recruiting talented remote workers is essential for building a successful remote team. Here are some tips to help you source and hire the best remote talent:

- ❖ Utilize job boards: There are several job boards that cater specifically to remote work, such as Remote.co, We Work Remotely, and Remote OK. These job boards allow businesses to advertise remote positions to a global audience and connect with prospective employees.

- ❖ Network on social media: LinkedIn and Twitter are great platforms for networking with potential remote workers. Businesses can join relevant groups or hashtags to connect with people who have similar interests or skills.

- ❖ Attend virtual career fairs: Virtual career fairs, such as those hosted by FlexJobs, are a great way to connect with remote workers and showcase your business to a global audience.

❖   Be clear on your requirements: When advertising for remote positions, be clear on the skills, experience, and personality traits that you are looking for. This will help to ensure that you attract the right candidates.

❖   Use skills tests: Skills tests are a great way to evaluate a candidate's abilities before hiring them. There are several platforms, such as Codility and TestDome, that offer skills tests for a range of job roles.

Interviewing and assessing potential remote employees

Once you have found prospective remote workers, it's crucial to interview and assess them effectively. Here are some tips to help you make the right hiring decision:

❖   Conduct video interviews: Video interviews allow you to get a sense of the candidate's personality and communication skills. They also help to establish a more personal connection with remote candidates.

❖   Assess their technical skills: If the position requires technical skills, ask the candidate to complete a technical task or skills test to verify their abilities.

❖   Assess their self-motivation: Working remotely requires a certain level of self-motivation and discipline. Ask the candidate to describe how they stay focused and productive while working from home.

❖   Assess their cultural fit: It's crucial to evaluate the candidate's cultural fit with your team. Ask questions about their working style, communication preferences, and how they approach collaboration.

Onboarding and training remote employees

Effective onboarding and training are essential to ensure that new remote employees feel integrated into the team and have the skills they need to perform their job. Here are some tips for onboarding and training remote employees:

❖ Set goals and expectations: Establish clear expectations for what the employee should achieve in their role and what is expected of them in terms of communication and availability.

❖ Provide a comprehensive onboarding package: Provide the employee with all the relevant onboarding materials and establish regular check-ins to ensure that they have everything they need.

❖ Develop a training plan: Develop a comprehensive training plan that covers all the skills and knowledge that the employee will need to perform the job effectively. Provide access to relevant training materials, such as online courses or tutorials.

❖ Emphasize communication: Communicate frequently with the employee and establish clear communication channels to ensure that they feel supported and connected to the team.

Managing remote employees' productivity and performance

Effective management is essential to ensure that remote employees remain productive and engaged. Here are some tips for managing remote employees' productivity and performance:

❖ Establish clear goals and expectations: Establish clear goals and expectations for each employee and communicate them regularly. This will help to ensure that everyone is working towards the same objectives.

❖ Use project management tools: Use project management

tools, such as Trello or Asana, to keep track of progress and assign tasks. These tools help to ensure that everyone is aware of their responsibilities and can manage their workload effectively.

❖ Establish regular check-ins: Schedule regular check-ins with each remote employee to discuss their progress and provide feedback. This will help to keep them motivated and ensure that they are on track to meet their goals.

❖ Use performance metrics: Use performance metrics to track each employee's productivity and identify areas for improvement. Metrics such as response time or completed tasks can help to measure remote employees' productivity.

Building a remote team culture

Building a team culture is crucial to ensure that remote employees feel connected to the business and their colleagues. Here are some tips for building a remote team culture:

❖ Hold virtual team-building events: Hold regular virtual team-building events, such as video calls or online games, to help employees feel connected to their colleagues.

❖ Use social media: Encourage employees to connect with each other on social media platforms, such as LinkedIn or Twitter. This can help to build a sense of community among remote employees.

❖ Emphasize communication: Effective communication is crucial to building a strong team culture. Encourage open communication channels and provide opportunities for regular feedback.

❖ Celebrate success: Celebrate success, both individual and team success, to help employees feel recognized and valued. This can help to build a positive team culture and increase employee satisfaction.

Avoiding common pitfalls in remote team management

Managing a remote team presents unique challenges, and it's crucial to avoid some common pitfalls. Here are some tips to help you avoid common pitfalls in remote team management:

❖ Avoid micromanagement: Micromanaging remote employees can lead to disengagement and reduced productivity. Trust your employees to manage their workload and provide support where needed.

❖ Establish clear communication channels: Establish clear communication channels to avoid misunderstandings and keep everyone on the same page.

❖ Address issues quickly: Address any issues or concerns promptly to avoid small problems becoming bigger issues.

❖ Avoid isolation: Encourage employees to connect with each other and the business regularly to avoid feelings of isolation or disconnection.

Conclusion

Managing a remote team presents unique challenges, but with the right approach, it can be a highly effective way to access a global talent pool and increase productivity. In this chapter, we explored the benefits of having a remote team, the challenges that come with managing a remote team, and how to recruit, onboard, and train remote workers effectively. By following best practices for remote team management and avoiding common pitfalls, businesses can build a successful remote team and take advantage of the benefits that come with remote work.

CHAPTER 7: OUTSOURCING FOR SMALL BUSINESSES

Small businesses are often faced with limited resources, which can hinder their ability to grow and compete with larger companies. Outsourcing can be a game-changer for small businesses, providing them with access to specialized skills and expertise they might not otherwise be able to afford. In this chapter, we'll explore the advantages and common outsourcing functions for small businesses, as well as best practices for finding and managing outsourcing partners.

Advantages of Outsourcing for Small Businesses

Small businesses often operate on tight budgets and with limited resources. Outsourcing can help small businesses overcome these limitations by providing access to specialized skills and expertise that might be cost-prohibitive to hire in-house. Here are some of the key advantages of outsourcing for small businesses:

❖ Cost Savings: Outsourcing can help small businesses save money on labor costs, office space, and equipment. Outsourcing partners can often provide these resources at a lower cost, allowing small businesses to allocate more funds towards other growth opportunities.

❖ Access to Specialized Skills: Outsourcing allows small

businesses to access expertise in areas where they might lack knowledge or experience, such as IT, accounting, or marketing. This can help small businesses compete with larger companies that have in-house specialists.

❖ Flexibility: Outsourcing can provide small businesses with the flexibility to scale up or down according to their needs. This means that small businesses can respond more quickly to market changes and adjust their resources accordingly.

❖ Increased Efficiency: Outsourcing can help small businesses streamline their operations and increase efficiency. Outsourcing partners can often provide faster turnaround times and higher quality work than an in-house team.

Common Outsourcing Functions for Small Businesses

Small businesses can outsource a wide range of functions, depending on their needs and goals. Here are some of the most common outsourcing functions for small businesses:

❖ Accounting and Bookkeeping: Small businesses can outsource their accounting and bookkeeping activities to third-party providers, allowing them to focus on their core business activities.

❖ IT Support: Small businesses can outsource their IT support needs, such as network management, software development, and database management, to technology companies.

❖ Digital Marketing: Small businesses can outsource their digital marketing activities, such as social media marketing, search engine optimization, and content creation, to digital marketing agencies.

❖ Human Resources: Small businesses can outsource

their human resources (HR) functions, such as payroll and benefits administration, recruitment, and training, to HR consultants or providers.

❖ Customer Service: Small businesses can outsource their customer service functions, such as call center operations and online chat support, to customer service providers.

Best Practices for Outsourcing for Small Businesses

Outsourcing can be a powerful tool for small businesses, but it requires careful planning and management to maximize its benefits. Here are some best practices for outsourcing for small businesses:

❖ Clearly Define Your Needs: Before seeking outsourcing partners, small businesses should clearly define their outsourcing needs and goals. This can help them identify the right partners and avoid common outsourcing mistakes.

❖ Research Potential Partners: Small businesses should research potential outsourcing partners thoroughly before making a decision. They should look for partners with experience in their industry and with a proven track record of delivering high-quality work.

❖ Create a Clear Contract: Small businesses should create a clear outsourcing contract that outlines the scope of work, timelines, deliverables, and payment terms. This can help avoid misunderstandings and disputes down the line.

❖ Communicate Effectively: Small businesses should establish clear communication channels with their outsourcing partners, including regular check-ins, progress reports, and feedback sessions. This can help ensure that the outsourcing relationship stays on track and any issues are addressed promptly.

❖ Build a Mutually Beneficial Relationship: Small businesses should approach outsourcing as a relationship, rather than a transaction. They should work to build strong relationships with their outsourcing partners based on trust, mutual respect, and open communication.

❖ Monitor Performance and Quality: Small businesses should regularly monitor their outsourcing partners' performance and quality of work. They should set clear performance metrics and goals and also provide feedback to help their outsourcing partners improve.

❖ Avoid Mistakes: Small businesses should learn from common outsourcing mistakes, such as underestimating the costs and risks of outsourcing, failing to communicate effectively, and choosing the wrong outsourcing partner.

Conclusion

Outsourcing can be a powerful tool for small businesses, providing them with access to specialized skills and expertise that might be cost-prohibitive to hire in-house. By carefully defining their outsourcing needs, researching potential partners, creating clear contracts, communicating effectively, building strong relationships, monitoring performance and quality, and avoiding common mistakes, small businesses can maximize the benefits of outsourcing and grow their businesses for long-term success.

CHAPTER 8:
OUTSOURCING
FOR STARTUPS

As a startup founder, you wear multiple hats and have many responsibilities. You are responsible for building a great product, acquiring users, creating a brand, and managing your finances, amongst other things. However, there is a limit to how many tasks you can take on by yourself, and you need a team to help you grow your business. Outsourcing can be a great way for startups to get the help they need without breaking the bank. In this chapter, we'll discuss how outsourcing can help startups grow and the best practices for outsourcing for startups.

Importance of Outsourcing for Startups

Startups by nature are often short on resources and have limited budgets. Therefore, it's crucial for them to be able to optimize the use of their resources and minimize costs wherever possible. Outsourcing can help startups achieve both of these objectives.

Outsourcing allows startups to access a pool of talent that they may not be able to afford to hire in-house. Outsourcing partners can offer specialized skills that you may not have on your team, such as marketing, customer support, or software development. These specialized skills can help you grow your business faster than if you were to try to develop them in-house.

Outsourcing also allows startups to access resources that they may not have in-house, such as equipment, software, or office space. By outsourcing, startups can avoid the costs of maintaining their own offices or equipment and only pay for the resources they need when they need them.

Finally, outsourcing can help startups save time, which is a precious resource for any startup founder. By outsourcing non-core tasks, such as accounting or administrative work, startups can focus on building their products and growing their businesses.

Common Outsourcing Functions for Startups

As a startup founder, you have to be strategic in deciding which tasks to outsource. Outsourcing can help you save time and money, but it's important to remember that outsourcing isn't a silver bullet that solves all your problems. Here are some common outsourcing functions that startups can consider:

❖ Software development: Outsourcing software development is common for startups because it allows them to leverage the expertise of developers without having to hire them in-house. Startups can outsource the development of their MVP (minimum viable product) or even their entire product to an outsourcing partner.

❖ Digital marketing: Startups need to acquire users and build their brand in order to grow. Outsourcing digital marketing can help startups get the expertise they need to create effective marketing campaigns, reach their target audience, and drive conversions.

❖ Customer support: Providing great customer support is critical for startups to retain customers and grow. Outsourcing customer support can help startups provide 24/7 support to their users without having to hire and manage a large team in-house.

❖   Accounting and bookkeeping: Startups need to keep their finances in order to succeed. Outsourcing accounting and bookkeeping functions can help startups keep their books up-to-date, manage cash flows, and produce financial reports.

❖   Administrative tasks: Administrative tasks such as data entry, scheduling, and email management may be time-consuming for startups. Outsourcing these tasks can help startups free up time to focus on more important tasks, such as product development or fundraising.

Best Practices for Outsourcing for Startups

Outsourcing can be a great way for startups to grow, but it's important to approach outsourcing strategically. Here are some best practices for outsourcing for startups:

❖   Identify your outsourcing needs: Before outsourcing any tasks, startups need to identify which tasks they need to outsource. Startups need to consider what tasks they can do in-house and which tasks they need help with. Prioritizing tasks by importance and urgency can help startups determine what tasks to outsource first.

❖   Find the right outsourcing partners: Finding the right outsourcing partner is critical for startups to succeed in outsourcing. Startups need to look for outsourcing partners that have experience working with startups and understand their unique needs. Startups should look for partners that are reliable, quality-driven, and have a proven track record.

❖   Manage outsourcing relationships effectively: Startups need to manage their outsourcing relationships effectively in order to get the most out of their outsourcing partnerships. Startups need to establish clear communication channels, set expectations and goals, monitor progress, and address any issues or concerns.

❖ Manage costs: Cost is a critical factor for startups, and they need to manage their outsourcing costs effectively. Startups should negotiate pricing and contracts with their outsourcing partners and look for cost-effective outsourcing strategies that meet their needs.

❖ Maintain control and oversight: While outsourcing can be a great way for startups to get the help they need, it's important for them to maintain control and oversight over their outsourcing partners. Startups need to ensure that their outsourcing partners are delivering quality work, meeting their deadlines, and adhering to their standards.

Risks and Benefits of Outsourcing for Startups

Outsourcing can be a great way for startups to grow, but it also comes with risks. Here are some benefits and risks of outsourcing for startups:

Benefits:

❖ Access to specialized skill sets: Outsourcing allows startups to access a pool of talent that they may not be able to afford to hire in-house. Outsourcing partners can offer specialized skills that startups may not have on their team, such as marketing, customer support, or software development.

❖ Cost savings: Outsourcing can help startups save money by avoiding the costs of hiring and maintaining an in-house team. By outsourcing non-core tasks, startups can focus on building their products and growing their businesses.

❖ Time savings: Outsourcing can help startups save time by allowing them to focus on their core competencies. By outsourcing non-core tasks, startups can free up time to focus on building their products and growing their businesses.

Risks:

❖ Quality control: One of the biggest risks of outsourcing is maintaining quality control over outsourced tasks. Startups need to ensure that their outsourcing partners are delivering quality work and adhering to their standards.

❖ Communication barriers: Communication barriers can be a challenge for startups that outsource tasks to partners in different time zones or countries. Startups need to establish clear communication channels and ensure that their outsourcing partners understand their requirements.

❖ Lack of control: Outsourcing can mean giving up some control over the work that is being done. Startups need to be comfortable with the level of control they are giving up when outsourcing tasks.

Incorporating Outsourcing into Your Startup's Growth Strategy

Outsourcing can be a powerful tool for startups to grow their businesses. However, it's important for startups to approach outsourcing strategically and with a clear plan. Here are some steps startups can take to incorporate outsourcing into their growth strategy:

❖ Identify which tasks to outsource: Start by identifying which tasks to outsource and which tasks to keep in-house. Prioritize the tasks by importance and urgency and create a plan for outsourcing them.

❖ Research potential outsourcing partners: Look for outsourcing partners that have experience working with startups and have a proven track record. Look for partners that are quality-driven, reliable, and cost-effective.

❖ Establish clear goals and expectations: Before starting any outsourcing relationship, establish clear goals and expectations. Make sure that both parties understand what is expected and what the timeline is.

❖ Communicate effectively: Communication is critical for successful outsourcing relationships. Establish clear communication channels and strive for open and transparent communication.

❖ Monitor progress and quality: Regularly monitor the progress and quality of outsourced tasks. Establish metrics for measuring success and ensure that outsourcing partners are meeting their deadlines and producing quality work.

❖ Adapt and refine your outsourcing strategy: Finally, be prepared to adapt and refine your outsourcing strategy, as necessary. Be open to feedback and make changes as needed.

Conclusion

Outsourcing can be a powerful tool for startups to grow their businesses and achieve their goals. By outsourcing non-core tasks, startups can free up time and resources to focus on building their products and acquiring customers. By understanding the benefits and risks of outsourcing and approaching outsourcing strategically, startups can achieve success and grow their businesses for the long-term.

CHAPTER 9: LEGAL CONSIDERATIONS IN OUTSOURCING

Outsourcing has become an integral part of doing business globally. Companies are increasingly turning to outsourcing to cut down costs, utilize expertise that they may not have, and to collaborate with third parties for holistic solutions. This growing trend has led to increased regulatory scrutiny, legal liabilities, and contract obligations that companies need to be aware of to avoid risks. This chapter covers the legal considerations that any organization should keep in mind before engaging in outsourcing, which will help you navigate the complex aspects of outsourcing legalities.

Understanding Legal Requirements for Outsourcing

Simply put, outsourcing is the act of hiring a third-party organization to complete a task that would typically be an in-house job. However, there are numerous legal obligations that need to be met before entering into an outsourcing agreement. To begin with, it's essential to consider local and international compliance laws - these should dictate the criteria for engaging outsourcing service providers. While laws and regulations differ depending on the country, generally, you must adhere to the legal obligations that are mandatory in your primary location and any other locations your outsourced provider operates. These legal obligations apply to documenting the relationship between your organization and the outsourced partner, including the nature of the outsourcing operation, time frame, scope, and any contractual agreements related to the engagement.

Structuring Outsourcing Contracts That Protect Both Parties

Outsourcing requires meticulous documentation - contracts and agreements, covering all the areas covered in the relationship, should be considered. Oral agreements are not sufficient in this regard. All outsourcing agreements must ensure that the parties involved in the agreement have a clear understanding of the tasks at hand. It's prudent to include information such as goals, time frames and particular details that relate to the task being outsourced, including delivery deadlines, costs, and breach clauses. Contracts should be signed by all parties in the agreement to acknowledge the terms and length of the relationship. As outsourcing keeps growing, laws on contractual agreement are continually evolving and as such, it's important that you consult with a qualified legal professional who is well versed in outsourcing agreements and the relevant laws.

Ensuring Compliance With Local Laws and Regulations

Outsourcing customers need to ensure that the outsourcing service providers meet all the necessary regulations governing their operations. Issues that outsourcing customers should take into account include retaining and removing customer data, adherence to labor law requirements, business licenses, security agreements, and the responsibility of intellectual property management. These legal obligations must be handled by the outsourcing service provider according to the stipulated time frames and conditions.

Mitigating Legal Risks Associated With Outsourcing

To mitigate the risks that come with outsourcing, it's imperative that organizations take a risk management approach that includes implementing effective policies, procedures, and training programs. Mitigation measures should be proactive since legal problems could arise, leading to potentially long and costly legal proceedings. As such, it's critical to involve legal experts who will keep you informed on the potential legal risks that may arise when outsourcing specific tasks. As with other business practices, successful outsourcing requires that you create a risk management plan that is consistent, continuous, and regularly-scheduled - to effectively mitigate any legal problems in the future.

Protecting Intellectual Property Rights During Outsourcing

Intellectual property rights, including trademarks, copyrights, patents, and other proprietary information are critical assets for businesses. While it's common to outsource non-core functions, intellectual property assets should never be sent outside the organization. Outsourcing service providers must sign specific agreements to protect the organization's intellectual property, and the outsourcing customer should review the contract carefully to ensure that their interests are well represented.

Addressing Privacy and Security Concerns in Outsourcing

Maintaining data privacy and security is a major aspect of outsourcing, and it's important for customers to ensure that their internal security policies are compatible with that of the outsourcing partner - this protects the organization from data loss and breaches, a growing concern in the modern age. Consequently, customers should be vigilant in reviewing security clauses in the outsourcing contract to make sure that the outsourced entity has implemented the necessary data loss prevention and security application processes.

Resolving Disputes and Breaches in Outsourcing Contracts

It's important for organizations to address potential disputes that may arise when outsourcing services. Before signing a contract, the parties involved need to discuss and agree to the terms of engagement fully. An effective way of managing potential disputes is by having clear, legal guidelines in place. The contracts should have dispute resolution clauses that are independent of jurisdictions, committees, and arbitrators. The agreement should clearly stipulate how these bodies will resolve disputes in case they arise.

Drafting Effective Contracts for Outsourcing Relationships

In conclusion, outsourcing can bring an organization significant benefits if managed well. As you will have noted, it's critical to cover all the legal aspects of outsourcing agreements. Unlike other business relationships, outsourcing relationships typically touch on intellectual property, privacy and security, and generally, execute sensitive tasks - hence the legal agreement should provide complete protection for both parties involved in entering the engagement. It's important to take the necessary time, engage legal professionals, and ensure that your agreement is reasonable and lawful so that you can enjoy a long-term, fruitful relationship with your outsourced partner.

CHAPTER 10: HUMAN RESOURCES OUTSOURCING

In today's rapidly changing business landscape, HR outsourcing has emerged as a popular option for organizations across industries. This chapter focuses on the benefits of HR outsourcing, best practices, and how to choose the right HR outsourcing partner. We also explore compliance laws and regulations, managing risks and issues, and measuring the ROI of HR outsourcing.

What is HR outsourcing?

HR outsourcing is defined as the process of delegation of HR functions to an external service provider, which helps manage HR processes, reduce costs, and improve overall efficiency. In simple terms, HR outsourcing involves hiring an external service provider to perform some or all of the HR functions of an organization so that the company can focus on its core competencies and business goals.

Benefits of HR outsourcing

There are numerous benefits of HR outsourcing that are driving the adoption of this practice worldwide. Some of the key benefits are:

❖   Cost savings: HR outsourcing helps companies minimize costs associated with employee salaries and benefits, as well as office space and equipment. Companies can eliminate the need to hire a full-time HR staff and only pay for what they need in terms of HR services.

❖   Strategic focus: Outsourcing HR frees up time for executives and HR departments to focus on strategic initiatives and core business goals.

❖   Access to expertise: HR outsourcing companies have the expertise to offer specialized HR services and support as and when needed.

❖   Flexibility and scalability: Organizations can leverage the expertise and resources of an HR outsourcing company to grow, scale, or downsize their business as needed.

Common HR outsourcing functions

HR outsourcing services can typically be categorized into the following areas:

❖ Recruitment and staffing

❖ HR administration and payroll

❖ Performance management

❖ Employee benefits

❖ Employee training and development

❖ Compliance management

❖ Employee relations and dispute resolution

Choosing the right HR outsourcing partner

When choosing an HR outsourcing partner, it is important to

consider a few key factors:

- ❖ Experience and reputation: Choosing an experienced and reputable HR outsourcing company is crucial to ensure quality services and a seamless outsourcing experience.

- ❖ Service offerings: It is important to ensure that the HR outsourcing provider offers the services you require and is able to customize their solutions to meet your specific needs.

- ❖ Industry expertise: Look for an HR outsourcing partner who has experience working within your particular industry, as they will be more adept at handling your unique HR requirements.

- ❖ Compliance and regulatory concerns: Choose an HR outsourcing company that is knowledgeable and compliant with federal and state labor laws, to help mitigate risks and avoid penalties down the line.

- ❖ Communication channels and accessibility: Effective communication and accessibility are crucial for successful outsourcing partnerships. Choose a partner that provides clear communication channels and is easily accessible in case of any issues or concerns.

Ensuring compliance with labor laws and regulations

Outsourcing HR functions does not absolve companies of their legal responsibilities when it comes to employment law compliance and regulatory requirements. It is important to ensure that HR outsourcing partners are knowledgeable and compliant with labor laws, to help mitigate risks and avoid penalties that can incur substantial costs. Companies should ensure that their HR outsourcing partners are following employment laws and regulations related to employee rights, benefits, and compensation such as:

❖ Fair Labor Standards Act (FLSA)

❖ Family and Medical Leave Act (FMLA)

❖ Americans with Disabilities Act (ADA)

❖ Occupational Safety and Health Act (OSHA)

❖ Equal Employment Opportunity Commission (EEOC)

❖ Employee Retirement Income Security Act (ERISA)

Mitigating HR risks associated with outsourcing

HR outsourcing may pose various risks that can affect a company's compliance, reputation, and overall business success. It is essential to have measures in place to mitigate these risks:

❖ Protecting confidential data: Companies should ensure that their HR outsourcing partners have adequate protection measures in place to prevent the loss or misuse of sensitive information.

❖ Contract management: Companies should establish clear and enforceable contracts to govern the outsourcing relationship, in order to avoid any misunderstandings or disputes.

❖ Cultural differences: Companies should be aware of possible cultural differences and potential misunderstandings between the outsourcing provider and their employees.

❖ Performance monitoring: Companies should monitor the performance of their outsourcing partners regularly and put in place metrics to measure their performance, to ensure that they are complying with the agreed-upon standards.

Managing HR outsourcing relationships effectively

Effective management and communication are critical to the success of HR outsourcing. It is important to establish a mutually beneficial and effective working relationship with the outsourcing partner to maximize the benefits of HR outsourcing. Some key practices in effective HR outsourcing management include:

❖   Clearly defining roles and responsibilities: Ensure that both parties have a clear understanding of their roles and responsibilities, and that these are reflected in the outsourcing agreement or contract.

❖   Maintaining regular communication: Regular communication and updates are crucial to ensure that the outsourcing relationship is on track and that any issues or concerns are promptly addressed.

❖   Monitoring performance and quality: Establishing metrics to measure performance and quality of services provided can help both parties monitor how well they are fulfilling their responsibilities.

❖   Managing cultural differences: HR outsourcing may involve working with teams across different geographical locations and cultures. Companies should be aware of possible cultural differences and find ways to ensure effective and respectful communication.

Measuring the ROI of HR outsourcing

Measuring the ROI of HR outsourcing is essential to understand the benefits of outsourcing and to evaluate its effectiveness. Companies can measure ROI in terms of:

❖   Cost savings: Companies should factor in the cost savings from HR outsourcing in terms of operational, administrative, and compliance-related expenses.

❖ Productivity gains: HR outsourcing can make HR processes more efficient, thereby freeing up time and resources for business growth and strategic activities.

❖ Improved quality: Outsourcing HR activities can help improve the level of quality and timeliness of services provided.

❖ Business impact: Companies should measure how outsourcing HR services has impacted their overall business performance, such as employee satisfaction, turnover rates, and revenue growth.

Conclusion

HR outsourcing can be a smart choice for companies seeking to focus on their core competencies, improve efficiency, and reduce costs. To make the most of HR outsourcing, companies must choose the right outsourcing partner, ensure compliance with labor laws and regulations, manage risks and issues, and effectively manage outsourcing relationships. Measuring the ROI of HR outsourcing can help companies evaluate the effectiveness of their outsourcing strategy and make informed decisions about future outsourcing initiatives.

CHAPTER 11: IT OUTSOURCING

IT outsourcing has become an increasingly popular business strategy for many organizations, allowing them to gain access to specialized expertise, reduce costs, and increase flexibility. In this chapter, we will explore the benefits and challenges of IT outsourcing, discuss common IT outsourcing functions, and provide guidance on how to choose the right IT outsourcing partner for your organization.

Definition of IT Outsourcing

IT outsourcing involves delegating some or all of an organization's IT operations to an external service provider. This can include functions such as software development, technical support, data center management, network and security management, and cloud computing services. IT outsourcing can be a cost-effective way to manage complex IT functions and reduce the burden on internal resources.

Benefits of IT Outsourcing

One of the main benefits of IT outsourcing is cost reduction. Rather than maintaining an in-house IT department, outsourcing IT functions can be significantly cheaper, particularly when it comes to tasks that require specialized expertise. This can also lead to increased efficiency, as outsourcing frees up internal resources to focus on core business functions.

Another advantage of IT outsourcing is access to specialized expertise. An outsourcing partner often has a team of experts with a broad knowledge base across different IT functions, which can be leveraged to improve the quality of service delivery. Outsourcing can also provide access to the latest technology and infrastructure, as outsourcing partners typically have access to advanced technologies and tools that may not be affordable for smaller organizations.

Common IT Outsourcing Functions

IT outsourcing functions can vary widely, based on the needs and requirements of a particular organization. Some of the most common IT outsourcing functions include:

❖ Software Development - Outsourcing software development can enable organizations to leverage specialized expertise, reduce costs, and bring products to market more quickly.

❖ Technical Support - Outsourcing technical support can free up internal resources and ensure that customers receive high-quality support around the clock.

❖ Data Center Management - Outsourcing data center management can improve data security and reduce the risk of downtime or data loss.

❖ Network and Security Management - Outsourcing network and security management can help organizations to reduce the risk of cyber-attacks and improve overall security posture.

❖ Cloud Computing Services - Outsourcing cloud services can provide access to cutting-edge infrastructure and technology, as well as on-demand scalability.

Choosing the Right IT Outsourcing Partner

Choosing the right IT outsourcing partner is critical to the success of the outsourcing initiative. Here are some key factors to consider when selecting an outsourcing partner:

❖ Expertise - Look for an outsourcing partner with deep expertise in the IT function you want to outsource. This can be verified through case studies, client references, and relevant certifications.

❖ Cost - Consider the overall cost of outsourcing, including both the direct costs and any potential hidden costs. Look for an outsourcing partner who offers transparent pricing and can help you estimate and control costs.

❖ Availability and Responsiveness - Choose an outsourcing partner who has the capacity to meet your needs and can provide responsive support when you need it.

❖ Communication and Collaboration - Effective communication is crucial when outsourcing IT functions. Look for an outsourcing partner who can offer clear communication channels and is willing to collaborate closely with your internal team.

❖ Security and Compliance - Data security and compliance are critical concerns in IT outsourcing. Choose an outsourcing partner who can demonstrate a strong track record of compliance and security and can provide relevant certifications as required.

Ensuring Data Security and Privacy in IT Outsourcing

One of the biggest concerns with IT outsourcing is data security and privacy. Companies that outsource their IT functions must take steps to ensure that sensitive data is protected and that contractual obligations are met. Here are some key steps to take to ensure data security and privacy in IT outsourcing:

❖ Define Security and Privacy Requirements - Clearly define your organization's security and privacy requirements, articulate them in the outsourcing contract, and ensure that your outsourcing partner meets those requirements.

❖ Conduct Background Checks - Conduct a thorough background check on any potential outsourcing partner to ensure that they have a clean record and no history of security breaches or legal violations.

❖ Use Secure Communication Channels - Use secure communication channels to exchange sensitive data and ensure that all data stored in the outsourcing partner's systems is encrypted.

❖ Include Security Provisions in the Contract - Include security provisions in the outsourcing contract, such as data encryption and access controls, to ensure that both parties are clear on their responsibilities.

❖ Conduct Regular Audits - Conduct regular audits of the outsourcing partner's security and privacy practices to ensure that they are in compliance with contractual obligations and industry standards.

Managing IT Outsourcing Relationships Effectively

Managing an IT outsourcing relationship effectively requires clear communication, careful planning, and regular monitoring. Here are some best practices for managing IT outsourcing relationships:

❖ Set Clear Expectations - Set clear expectations and goals for the outsourcing relationship and define roles and responsibilities for both the outsourcing partner and internal team members.

❖ Establish Regular Communication - Establish regular

communication channels and schedules and ensure that both parties have access to the information they need to make effective decisions.

❖ Monitor Performance and Quality - Set up metrics to monitor the outsourcing partner's performance and quality and establish a process for addressing any issues or concerns.

❖ Build Trust - Building trust is critical to a successful outsourcing relationship. Establish a culture of transparency and collaboration and be proactive in addressing any issues that arise.

❖ Develop Contingency Plans - Develop contingency plans to address potential risks, such as data breaches or service disruptions, and define the steps that will be taken in the event of a crisis.

Measuring the ROI of IT Outsourcing

Measuring the ROI of IT outsourcing can be a complex task, but it is critical to establishing the value of the outsourcing relationship. Here are some key metrics to consider when measuring the ROI of IT outsourcing:

❖ Cost Savings - Calculate the cost savings achieved through outsourcing, including direct costs such as labor and equipment, as well as indirect costs such as improved efficiency and reduced downtime.

❖ Quality Metrics - Track quality metrics, such as customer satisfaction and error rates, to determine whether outsourcing has led to improvements in service delivery.

❖ Time to Market - Measure the time it takes to bring products and services to market and assess whether outsourcing has helped to reduce time to market.

❖ Expertise and Innovation - Assess whether outsourcing has provided access to new expertise or innovative solutions that would not have been possible with an in-house team.

❖ Flexibility - Measure the flexibility and scalability achieved through outsourcing and assess whether it has helped the organization to respond more quickly to changing business needs.

Conclusion

IT outsourcing can be a powerful strategy for organizations looking to reduce costs, increase efficiency, and gain access to specialized expertise. By following best practices for choosing an outsourcing partner, ensuring data security and privacy, managing outsourcing relationships effectively, and measuring the ROI of IT outsourcing, organizations can achieve long-term success and maximize the benefits of outsourcing.

CHAPTER 12: OUTSOURCING FOR NON-PROFIT ORGANIZATIONS

Outsourcing has become increasingly popular among non-profit organizations due to the numerous benefits it offers. Non-profit organizations face unique challenges such as limited resources, tight budgets, and a constant need to deliver on their mission and objectives. Outsourcing can help non-profit organizations overcome these challenges and accomplish more with less.

Common Outsourcing Functions for Non-Profits

Non-profit organizations can outsource various functions to improve their operations and effectiveness. These include:

❖ Accounting and Bookkeeping: Non-profits need to maintain accurate financial records to comply with government regulations and to track donations and expenses. Outsourcing accounting and bookkeeping functions can help ensure that financial records are accurate, timely, and compliant.

❖ Fundraising: Fundraising is critical for non-profits to maintain their programs and initiatives. Outsourcing fundraising can help non-profits tap into expertise, resources, and networks they may not have in-house.

❖ IT Services: Non-profits rely on technology to manage their operations, communicate with donors and partners, and deliver their programs. Outsourcing IT services can help non-profits access the technology and expertise they need to operate efficiently and effectively.

❖ Marketing and Communications: Non-profits need to promote their cause and engage donors and supporters to raise awareness and funding. Outsourcing marketing and communications can help non-profits reach a broader audience and promote their mission without investing significant resources.

Best Practices for Outsourcing for Non-Profits

Non-profit organizations need to approach outsourcing strategically to ensure they get the right services and outcomes. The following best practices can help non-profits maximize the benefits of outsourcing:

❖ Define Your Needs: Non-profits need to identify the specific functions or services they want to outsource and the outcomes they want to achieve. This will help them create a clear scope of work and set expectations with their outsourcing partners.

❖ Research Potential Partners: Non-profits need to conduct thorough research to find outsourcing partners that have experience working with non-profit organizations and offer the services they need. They should also assess their credibility, expertise, and reputation before entering into an outsourcing relationship.

❖ Evaluate Performance Metrics: Non-profit organizations need to establish performance metrics to measure the effectiveness of their outsourcing relationships. This can include tracking specific outcomes, such as donor engagement, cost savings, and efficiency gains.

❖ Establish Effective Communication Channels: Non-profit organizations need to ensure effective communication with their outsourcing partners to maintain a transparent and productive relationship. This involves setting up regular meetings, calls, and reporting systems to track progress and address issues promptly.

❖ Build a Strong Relationship: Non-profit organizations need to establish a strong and mutually beneficial relationship with their outsourcing partners. This involves building trust, fostering transparency, and promoting open communication to ensure the outsourcing relationship delivers the desired outcomes.

Cost-Effective Outsourcing Strategies for Non-Profits

Non-profit organizations can adopt various cost-effective outsourcing strategies to maximize the benefits of outsourcing while keeping costs under control. These include:

❖ Negotiate Pricing: Non-profit organizations can negotiate pricing and contracts with their outsourcing partners to get the services they need at a reasonable cost.

❖ Consider Shared Services: Non-profit organizations can share services with other non-profit entities to achieve cost savings and increase efficiency. This can involve sharing back-office functions, such as accounting, IT, and HR.

❖ Leverage Volunteer Services: Non-profit organizations can leverage volunteer services to supplement their outsourcing activities. This can help them save costs while tapping into the expertise and experience of volunteers.

❖ Use Crowdsourcing: Non-profit organizations can use

crowdsourcing platforms to source solutions to specific problems or challenges. This can help them access a broad range of expertise and perspectives at a low cost.

Risks and Benefits of Outsourcing for Non-Profits

Outsourcing can provide numerous benefits for non-profit organizations, such as improved efficiency, cost savings, access to expertise, and increased capacity. However, outsourcing also poses some risks and challenges, such as language barriers, cultural differences, loss of control, and quality issues. Non-profit organizations need to assess their outsourcing needs and risks carefully before entering into an outsourcing relationship.

Incorporating Outsourcing into Non-Profit's Growth Strategy

Outsourcing can play a critical role in helping non-profit organizations achieve their mission and grow sustainably. Non-profit organizations need to incorporate outsourcing into their growth strategy by identifying the specific functions or services they want to outsource, finding the right outsourcing partners, establishing communication channels, and measuring performance outcomes. By adopting a strategic approach to outsourcing, non-profit organizations can achieve their objectives more efficiently and effectively.

CHAPTER 13: OUTSOURCING IN HEALTHCARE

Outsourcing has become a popular strategy for healthcare organizations in recent years. The benefits of outsourcing in healthcare include cost savings, improved efficiency, access to specialized expertise, and the ability to focus on core business functions. The following are common healthcare functions that can be outsourced:

❖   Revenue cycle management (RCM) – This includes medical billing, coding, claims processing, and collections. Outsourcing RCM can help healthcare organizations save time and money while improving revenue and cash flow.

❖   Medical transcription – This involves converting voice-recorded reports into written documents. Outsourcing medical transcription can save healthcare organizations time and help improve accuracy.

❖   Medical coding – This includes assigning codes to medical diagnoses and procedures for billing purposes. Outsourcing medical coding can improve accuracy and compliance, as well as reduce errors and denials.

❖   Health information management (HIM) – This involves managing electronic health records (EHRs), privacy and security, and data analytics. Outsourcing HIM can help healthcare organizations improve data quality and utilization, as well as reduce costs.

Choosing the right healthcare outsourcing partner is critical to the success of outsourcing initiatives. Here are some factors to consider:

- ❖ Industry experience – Look for a vendor that has experience working with healthcare organizations and understands the unique challenges and regulations in the industry.

- ❖ Quality and compliance – Look for a vendor that has established quality assurance processes and compliance with industry regulations such as HIPAA.

- ❖ Technology infrastructure – Look for a vendor that has a reliable and secure technology infrastructure to manage data.

- ❖ Customer service – Look for a vendor that has a dedicated customer service team to address any issues or concerns.

- ❖ Pricing – Look for a vendor that offers competitive pricing and a flexible pricing model.

Once you have chosen a healthcare outsourcing partner, it's important to ensure compliance with healthcare laws and regulations, including HIPAA. Here are some tips for managing healthcare outsourcing relationships:

- ❖ Define roles and responsibilities – Establish clear roles and responsibilities for both parties, including communication protocols, escalation procedures, and reporting requirements.

- ❖ Build a culture of trust and transparency – Establish a relationship based on trust and transparency, which includes regular communication and open feedback.

❖ Monitor performance and outcomes – Set performance metrics and outcomes, and regularly monitor and evaluate performance to ensure the outsourcing partner is meeting expectations.

❖ Address issues and concerns in a timely manner – Proactively address any issues or concerns that arise in the outsourcing relationship to prevent them from becoming bigger problems.

❖ Develop a contingency plan – Develop a contingency plan in case of any disruptions or issues that may impact the outsourcing relationship.

In conclusion, outsourcing in healthcare can provide significant benefits to healthcare organizations, but it's important to choose the right outsourcing partner and manage the outsourcing relationship effectively to ensure compliance, quality, and performance. By following best practices in outsourcing, healthcare organizations can improve efficiency, reduce costs, and focus on providing high-quality patient care.

CHAPTER 14: ACCOUNTING AND FINANCE OUTSOURCING

Outsourcing accounting and finance functions has become increasingly popular in recent years. Both small and large businesses have started to recognize the benefits of outsourcing these functions, including cost savings, increased efficiency, and access to specialized expertise. In this chapter, we will explore the benefits and challenges of outsourcing accounting and finance functions and provide practical tips for managing outsourcing relationships effectively.

Benefits of Accounting and Finance Outsourcing

Accounting and finance outsourcing can provide businesses with several benefits, including:

- ❖ Cost savings: Outsourcing accounting and finance functions can be a cost-effective alternative to hiring full-time employees. Businesses can save on employment benefits and salaries, while having access to skilled accounting and finance professionals.

- ❖ Increased efficiency: Outsourcing accounting and finance functions can free up time for businesses to focus on their core activities. This can lead to increased efficiency, productivity, and profitability.

❖   Access to specialized expertise: Outsourcing accounting and finance functions provides businesses with access to specialized expertise that they may not have in-house. This includes expertise in tax compliance, financial reporting, and accounting software.

Common Accounting and Finance Outsourcing Functions

Businesses can outsource a wide range of accounting and finance functions, including:

❖   Bookkeeping: Outsourcing bookkeeping involves outsourcing the day-to-day management of financial transactions, including billing, accounts payable, and accounts receivable.

❖   Payroll processing: Outsourcing payroll processing involves outsourcing the processing of employee payroll, including payments, taxes, and reporting.

❖   Tax preparation: Outsourcing tax preparation involves outsourcing the preparation of tax returns for businesses, including income tax, sales tax, and payroll tax.

❖   Financial reporting: Outsourcing financial reporting involves outsourcing the preparation of financial statements, balance sheets, and income statements, among others.

❖   Controller services: Outsourcing controller services involves outsourcing the management of accounting operations, including analysis of financial data and reporting to management.

Choosing the Right Accounting and Finance Outsourcing

Partner

When choosing an accounting and finance outsourcing partner, it is essential to research potential partners thoroughly. The following are some factors to consider when choosing an outsourcing partner:

❖ Expertise: Choose a partner with expertise in the particular accounting and finance functions you need outsourced.

❖ Reputation: Choose a partner with a strong reputation in the industry and ask for references to confirm their track record.

❖ Service-level agreement: Choose a partner with a clear and comprehensive service-level agreement (SLA) that outlines the scope of the outsourcing relationship, including the services to be provided, turnaround times, and quality standards.

❖ Flexibility: Choose a partner that can adapt to changing needs and provide services on an as-needed basis.

❖ Data security: Choose a partner with robust data security and privacy policies in place to protect sensitive financial information.

Ensuring Compliance with Accounting and Finance Laws and Regulations

Outsourcing accounting and finance functions requires businesses to comply with various laws and regulations. Compliance with these laws and regulations can be challenging, especially when outsourcing partners are located in different jurisdictions. Here are some tips for ensuring compliance with accounting and finance laws and regulations:

❖ Research local requirements: Research the legal and regulatory requirements of the local jurisdiction where the outsourcing partner is located.

❖ Agree on compliance measures: Ensure that the outsourcing partner is aware of the legal and regulatory requirements and agrees to take adequate measures to comply with them.

❖ Regular audits: Conduct regular audits to ensure that the outsourcing partner is complying with all legal and regulatory requirements.

❖ Compliance reporting: Require the outsourcing partner to provide regular compliance reports that demonstrate their compliance with all legal and regulatory requirements.

❖ Contractual obligations: Ensure that the outsourcing contract includes clear and specific obligations and warranties regarding compliance with laws and regulations.

Mitigating Accounting and Finance Risks Associated with Outsourcing

There are several risks associated with outsourcing accounting and finance functions. These include data security breaches, financial fraud, and errors in financial reporting. Here are some tips for mitigating these risks:

❖ Risk assessment: Conduct a risk assessment to identify potential risks related to outsourcing accounting and finance functions.

❖ Background checks: Screen the outsourcing partner to ensure that they have a clean record and no history of financial fraud or data breaches.

❖ Data security: Implement robust data security measures to protect sensitive financial information.

❖ Fraud prevention: Implement robust fraud prevention measures to detect and prevent financial fraud.

❖ Quality control: Implement quality control measures to ensure that financial data is accurate and reliable.

Managing Accounting and Finance Outsourcing Relationships Effectively

Managing accounting and finance outsourcing relationships requires clear communication, regular monitoring, and effective performance management. Here are some tips for managing outsourcing relationships effectively:

❖ Establish lines of communication: Establish clear lines of communication with the outsourcing partner, including reporting requirements and communication channels.

❖ Monitor performance: Monitor the outsourcing partner's performance regularly to ensure that they are meeting the agreed-upon service levels and quality standards.

❖ Address issues promptly: Address any issues or concerns that arise promptly and work collaboratively with the outsourcing partner to resolve them.

❖ Review results: Regularly review the results of the outsourcing relationship and measure the return on investment (ROI).

❖ Renew and continue: Renew the outsourcing relationship if it is working well and continue to refine the relationship to achieve better results.

Conclusion

Outsourcing accounting and finance functions can provide businesses with several benefits, including cost savings, increased efficiency, and access to specialized expertise. However, managing outsourcing relationships requires careful planning, clear communication, and effective performance management. With the right outsourcing partner and effective management strategies, businesses can achieve long-term success and growth.

CHAPTER 15: MARKETING AND ADVERTISING OUTSOURCING

Marketing and advertising are crucial components of any business, as they help in creating brand awareness and attracting potential customers. Outsourcing marketing and advertising functions have become increasingly popular among businesses due to the numerous benefits associated with it.

Benefits of Marketing and Advertising Outsourcing:

1. Cost Savings:

Marketing and advertising require a substantial investment of time and money, but outsourcing can significantly reduce both of these expenses. By partnering with an outsourcing company, businesses can benefit from the economies of scale, as the outsourcing provider can leverage their expertise and buying power to get better pricing for media and other advertising services.

2. Access to Expertise:

Marketing and advertising outsourcing companies specialize

in these functions and have the necessary expertise, skills, and experience to deliver high-quality results. By outsourcing these functions, businesses can tap into diverse expertise to devise effective marketing strategies, create compelling content, optimize campaigns, and track and analyze results to continuously improve their marketing efforts.

3. Scalability:

Outsourcing marketing and advertising functions are especially beneficial for businesses that experience seasonal fluctuations, as they can scale up or down their marketing and advertising efforts based on demand without incurring additional fixed costs. This flexibility can be an enormous advantage for businesses that need to quickly pivot their strategy to adapt to changes in the competitive landscape or customer preferences.

4. Focus on Core Competencies:

By outsourcing marketing and advertising, businesses can focus on their core competencies and strategic objectives while the outsourcing partner handles daily marketing operations. This shift in workload can free up time and resources for businesses to focus on their business's growth and profitability.

Common Marketing and Advertising Outsourcing Functions:

1. Content Creation:

Content creation is a critical component of any marketing and advertising strategy, and outsourcing companies can provide businesses with a range of content creation services, such as article writing, video creation, infographics, social media posts, email marketing, and more.

2. Digital Marketing:

Digital marketing has become the most preferred marketing and advertising channel among businesses. Outsourcing companies can provide businesses with a range of digital marketing services, such as search engine optimization (SEO), search engine marketing (SEM), paid social media advertising, email marketing, and more.

3. Public Relations:

Public relations (PR) is another common function that businesses outsource to an external partner. PR outsourcing companies provide businesses with a range of services, such as press releases, media outreach, crisis management, and more.

Choosing the Right Marketing and Advertising Outsourcing Partner:

1. Experience and Expertise:

When choosing a marketing and advertising outsourcing partner, businesses should consider the outsourcing company's experience and expertise. The outsourcing partner should have a track record of delivering quality services and have the necessary expertise to handle their specific industry and market.

2. Proof of Concept:

A reputable outsourcing company should be able to provide businesses with proof of concept, which is a demonstration of their past successes. Businesses can ask for references, case studies, and performance metrics to determine if the outsourcing company has a suitable track record of success.

3. Communication:

It is essential to establish clear communication channels, reporting, and tracking mechanisms at the outset of the outsourcing relationship. A successful outsourcing relationship depends on effective communication between a business and their outsourcing partner.

4. Cost and Budget:

One of the most significant benefits of outsourcing marketing and advertising functions is cost savings. However, businesses should still establish mutually agreed-upon costs and expectations upfront to avoid any surprises.

Managing Marketing and Advertising Outsourcing Relationships Effectively:

1. Clear Expectations and Goals:

Outsourcing companies' success depends on clear expectations and goals from companies. Businesses should set goals and metrics upfront to ensure that both parties have a clear understanding of their expectations and that all deliverables are met collaboratively.

2. Constant Communication:

Outsourcing requires constant communication to ensure that employees' skills and the provided resources meet the business's goals and objectives. A good outsourcing partner should have an established process for providing progress reports and real-time updates to keep businesses informed.

3. Performance Metrics:

Performance metrics are critical to measuring the effectiveness of outsourcing marketing and advertising functions. These metrics should be established upfront to track progress and identify opportunities for improvement.

4. Addressing Issues and Concerns:

When outsourcing marketing and advertising functions, issues may arise, which should be addressed promptly to prevent any adverse impact on business operations.

Building a Strong Brand Identity through Marketing and Advertising Outsourcing:

A strong brand identity is essential for businesses to stand out in a crowded market. By outsourcing marketing and advertising functions, businesses can leverage their partner's expertise and experience to create a unique brand identity that resonates with their target audience.

In conclusion, outsourcing marketing and advertising functions can significantly benefit businesses by delivering cost savings, access to expertise, scalability, and allowing businesses to focus on their core competencies. However, it is crucial to choose the right outsourcing partner carefully, establish clear expectations and goals, maintain ongoing communication, use performance metrics to monitor progress, and address any issues or concerns promptly to ensure the outsourcing relationship's success.

CHAPTER 16: CUSTOMER SUPPORT OUTSOURCING

In today's corporate environment, providing excellent customer support is no longer optional, it is essential. With customer demand and expectations only increasing, businesses know that they cannot solely rely on providing quality products and services to attract and retain customers. Rather, building a reputation for top-notch customer support is paramount. However, not every organization has the resources or expertise in-house to provide exceptional customer support. This is where customer support outsourcing comes in.

Benefits of Customer Support Outsourcing

The most significant advantage of outsourcing customer support is that businesses can focus on their core competencies while leaving customer support to the experts. Besides, outsourcing customer support can provide a cost-effective solution, as businesses can save on expenses related to recruiting and training in-house customer support agents. This is often beneficial for small and medium-sized enterprises that require customer support but do not have the resources to set up a dedicated team in-house.

Common Customer Support Outsourcing Functions

There are several functions that businesses can outsource to third-party providers when it comes to customer support services. These include but are not limited to:

❖ Inbound customer service calls

❖ Email and chat support

❖ Technical support

❖ Product and order inquiry management

❖ Help desk and ticket management

Choosing the Right Customer Support Outsourcing Partner

One of the most critical decisions when it comes to outsourcing customer support is choosing the right partner. After all, customer support is synonymous with the brand image of an organization, and a wrong choice in outsourcing can lead to a bad reputation and lost business.

When choosing a customer support outsourcing partner, consider factors such as the provider's experience and expertise in providing customer support in your industry. Be sure to ask for references and find out what other customers have to say about their experience with the provider. Additionally, ensure that the provider has the capacity to handle the volume of customer support that your business requires. Finally, ensure that the provider has a robust quality control process in place so that they can deliver the level of customer support that your business requires.

Ensuring Compliance with Customer Support Laws and Regulations

When outsourcing customer support, businesses must ensure

that their customer support outsourcing partner complies with all laws and regulations that apply to customer support. One example is the Telephone Consumer Protection Act (TCPA), which limits telemarketing calls and texts made using automatic telephone dialing systems. It is essential to ensure that an outsourcing partner complies with all applicable laws and regulations to mitigate legal risk.

Mitigating Customer Support Risks Associated with Outsourcing

As with any outsourcing relationship, there are risks associated with customer support outsourcing that must be mitigated. One of these risks is the loss of control over customer support experience. To prevent this, businesses must provide clear guidelines and detailed instructions to outsourcing partners. Additionally, businesses must ensure that their customer support outsourcing providers are adequately trained on the organization's products, services, and brand identity.

Managing Customer Support Outsourcing Relationships Effectively

The key to successful customer support outsourcing is managing the relationship effectively. This requires an effective communication system to ensure that communication is clear, concise, and timely. Regular performance reviews and quality control checks must also be conducted to identify and rectify any issues that may arise.

Measuring the ROI of Customer Support Outsourcing

As with any business investment, it is essential to measure the ROI of customer support outsourcing. Two critical metrics that can be used to evaluate customer support outsourcing are customer satisfaction surveys and cost savings. By tracking these metrics, businesses can identify the impact of their customer support outsourcing initiatives and make informed decisions about the future of their outsourcing strategy.

Building Customer Loyalty through Effective Customer Support Outsourcing

Customer support outsourcing can be an essential tool in building customer loyalty. By providing outstanding customer support experiences, businesses can increase customer satisfaction and retention while building the reputation of their brand. When selecting a customer support outsourcing partner, businesses must ensure that the provider shares their vision and values to provide a consistent customer experience.

Conclusion

Outsourcing customer support can be a cost-effective and efficient solution for businesses looking to provide top-notch customer support. However, it is essential to choose the right outsourcing partner, ensure compliance with laws and regulations, mitigate risks, manage the relationship effectively, and measure ROI. By following these best practices, businesses can build a reputation for exceptional customer support while focusing on their core competencies.

CHAPTER 17: OUTSOURCING FOR GOVERNMENT AGENCIES

In recent years, government agencies have increasingly turned to outsourcing as a way to cut costs, improve service delivery, and streamline operations. Outsourcing can be particularly attractive to government agencies that are facing budget constraints, staff shortages, or technological challenges. In this chapter, we will explore the benefits, risks, and best practices of outsourcing for government agencies.

Benefits of Outsourcing for Government Agencies

Outsourcing can offer a range of benefits for government agencies, including:

❖   Cost savings: By outsourcing certain functions, government agencies can reduce overhead costs associated with staffing, training, and maintaining infrastructure.

❖   Improved service delivery: Outsourcing can help government agencies improve the quality and efficiency of their services by tapping into the expertise and resources of specialized service providers.

❖ Increased flexibility: Outsourcing can give government agencies more flexibility to scale up or down their services in response to changing demands or budgets.

❖ Access to new technologies: Outsourcing can provide government agencies with access to new technologies without requiring significant upfront investments in hardware, software, or training.

❖ Reduced risk: Outsourcing can help government agencies mitigate risk by relying on the expertise and experience of service providers who have already established best practices and standards.

Common Outsourcing Functions for Government Agencies

Government agencies outsource a wide range of functions, including:

❖ Information Technology (IT): IT outsourcing can include help desk and technical support services, infrastructure management, software development, and data center operations.

❖ Procurement: Procurement outsourcing can include vendor management, contract management, and procurement operations.

❖ Human Resources (HR): HR outsourcing can include payroll processing, benefits administration, talent management, and recruitment.

❖ Facilities Management: Facilities management outsourcing can include maintenance, repairs, cleaning, and security.

❖ Communications: Communications outsourcing can include public relations, media relations, marketing, and advertising.

Best Practices for Outsourcing for Government Agencies

When outsourcing, government agencies need to follow certain best practices, including:

* ❖ Define clear goals and objectives: Before embarking on outsourcing, government agencies should define clear goals and objectives that align with their strategic vision.

* ❖ Select the right outsourcing partner: Government agencies should carefully evaluate potential outsourcing partners based on their expertise, experience, reputation, and financial stability.

* ❖ Develop a comprehensive outsourcing contract: Government agencies should develop a comprehensive outsourcing contract that includes clear performance metrics, service level agreements (SLAs), and dispute resolution procedures.

* ❖ Establish effective communication channels: Government agencies should establish effective communication channels with their outsourcing partners to ensure that information is exchanged in a timely and accurate manner.

* ❖ Monitor performance and results: Government agencies should monitor the performance and results of their outsourcing partners on an ongoing basis to ensure that they are meeting their contractual obligations and delivering value.

* ❖ Manage cultural and ethical risks: Government agencies should be sensitive to cultural and ethical differences when outsourcing to ensure that the rights and interests of all parties are protected.

* ❖ Stay informed about outsourcing trends and best practices: Government agencies should stay informed about the latest

outsourcing trends and best practices to continuously refine their outsourcing strategies and initiatives.

Risks and Challenges of Outsourcing for Government Agencies

While outsourcing can offer significant benefits for government agencies, it is not without its risks and challenges, including:

❖   Loss of control: Outsourcing can result in reduced control over certain functions and activities, which can be a concern for some government agencies.

❖   Quality issues: Poor quality or substandard service delivery can damage the reputation of government agencies and erode public trust.

❖   Security and privacy concerns: Government agencies need to ensure that sensitive information is protected during outsourcing and that appropriate measures are taken to safeguard data security and privacy.

❖   Compliance issues: Government agencies need to ensure that outsourcing partners comply with applicable laws, regulations, and standards.

❖   Vendor lock-in: Government agencies must be cautious when entering into long-term contracts with outsourcing partners that may lead to vendor lock-in or dependence.

Cost-effective Outsourcing Strategies for Government Agencies

Government agencies can adopt a range of cost-effective outsourcing strategies, including:

❖   Collaborative outsourcing: Collaborative outsourcing involves partnering with other government agencies or private sector organizations to leverage economies of scale and shared resources.

❖ Selective outsourcing: Selective outsourcing involves outsourcing specific functions or activities where outsourcing can deliver the greatest value.

❖ Multi-sourcing: Multi-sourcing involves engaging with multiple outsourcing partners to divide workloads and avoid vendor lock-in.

❖ Nearshoring/offshoring: Nearshoring/offshoring involves outsourcing to service providers in nearby or overseas locations where costs are lower.

Incorporating Outsourcing into Your Government Agency's Growth Strategy

To successfully incorporate outsourcing into your government agency's growth strategy, you need to:

❖ Conduct a comprehensive analysis of your existing operations to identify areas where outsourcing can deliver the greatest value.

❖ Develop a clear outsourcing strategy and action plan that aligns with your government agency's strategic goals and objectives.

❖ Identify the right outsourcing partners who have the necessary expertise, experience, and financial stability.

❖ Establish clear lines of communication and performance monitoring mechanisms to ensure that outsourcing partners deliver on their contractual obligations.

❖ Always be aware of the potential risks and challenges of outsourcing and take appropriate steps to mitigate them.

Conclusion

Outsourcing can be an effective tool for government agencies to cut costs, improve service delivery, and streamline operations. By following best practices, mitigating risks, and adopting cost-effective outsourcing strategies, government agencies can effectively leverage outsourcing to deliver more value to their constituents and stakeholders.

CHAPTER 18: CULTURAL AND ETHICAL CONSIDERATIONS IN OUTSOURCING

Outsourcing, like any other business model, has its cultural and ethical nuances, which can have a lasting impact on your business success. Outsourcing helps companies expand their reach into international markets and tap into a global workforce, but at the same time, it demands a sensitive approach when it comes to cultural differences and ethical considerations. In this chapter, we will explore the significant cultural and ethical risks that can arise during outsourcing and how to manage them effectively.

Understanding Cultural Differences in Outsourcing

Culture is the sum of values, beliefs, social norms, and customs that define a group of people's way of life. When doing business across borders, you are dealing with cultures that can differ significantly in how they perceive work, communication, and business relationships. In outsourcing, it's essential to understand that these cultural differences can impact your outsourcing experience. For instance, cultural differences can affect the communication style, work ethic, and decision-making processes of your outsourcing partner.

To successfully navigate cultural differences, you need to be sensitive to cultural norms and customs. Taking time to understand your outsourcing partner's cultural background is key in building trust and a positive working relationship. Inclusivity and diversity play a significant role in bridging the cultural divide while outsourcing. By cultivating an understanding of different cultural backgrounds, you can leverage that knowledge to create an inclusive and welcoming outsourcing team.

Addressing Ethical Concerns in Outsourcing

Ethical concerns are among the major challenges of outsourcing. Companies that outsource must ensure that their outsourcing partner adheres to ethical standards when operating in different locations. Ethical concerns may include the treatment of employees, exploitation of cheap labor, and intellectual property theft.

While outsourcing can reduce operating costs, companies must not compromise ethical concerns in search of cheap labor and sweatshops. The exploitation of cheap labor can harm an outsourcing partner's reputation and negatively impact your business, resulting in lost contracts and revenue. Therefore, it's important to ensure that your outsourcing partner operates ethically by adhering to set industry standards and treating employees with fairness.

Building Cross-cultural Relationships with Outsourcing Partners

Building cross-cultural relationships is a critical aspect of successful outsourcing. Cross-cultural relationships entail finding common ground across different cultures, gaining cultural competence, and encouraging a shared sense of purpose. Cross-cultural relationships lay the foundation for a positive and productive relationship with your outsourcing partner.

Effective communication is key when building cross-cultural relationships while outsourcing. It's important to ensure that both parties communicate well and understand each other's business norms and customs. Communication is critical, as it helps to overcome the language barrier, bridge cultural differences and create a more inclusive and responsive outsourcing team.

Ensuring Ethical Behavior Throughout the Outsourcing Process

To ensure ethical behavior throughout the outsourcing process, it's essential that both parties agree on ethical standards that align with industry best practices. Once your outsourcing partner is on board, you can create an ethics policy that sets out the ethical standards in your outsourcing relationship. The ethics policy should be a written document included in the outsourcing contract and should be communicated clearly to all parties.

It's important to monitor your outsourcing partner's ethical behavior throughout the outsourcing process. Regular site visits, auditing, and ensuring compliance with industry standards can help you gauge your outsourcing partner's ethical behavior. Mitigating cultural and ethical risks associated with outsourcing requires a collaborative approach that involves a shared understanding of ethical values.

Managing Cultural and Ethical Risks Associated with Outsourcing

Managing cultural and ethical risks requires a proactive approach that begins with understanding the cultural nuances and ethical standards associated with outsourcing. Effective management of cultural and ethical risks entails mitigating risks by implementing ethical standards in the outsourcing relationship, building cross-cultural relationships, and ensuring regular communication and monitoring of ethical behavior.

To effectively manage cultural and ethical risks, it is essential to have a robust system for identify issues. This means having clear reporting mechanisms that allow for timely identification and reporting of any potential cultural or ethical violations. Regular communication between both parties can help identify potential risks early on and address them before they become bigger issues.

Staying Ahead of the Curve in Outsourcing

The outsourcing industry is an evolving industry, with emerging technologies and trends that can impact outsourcing decisions. Staying informed about the latest developments and best practices is essential in managing cultural and ethical risks. Developing a comprehensive outsourcing strategy, such as sourcing models and developing sourcing partners, can help you stay ahead of the curve in outsourcing.

In conclusion, outsourcing is not just a business model; it's a way of life for companies who want to be competitive in a global market. With a sensitive approach to cultural differences and ethical considerations, you can build successful outsourcing relationships that can deliver a long-term strategic advantage. By creating an understanding of ethical considerations and cultural differences, you can foster a positive and productive partnership with your outsourcing partner, mitigating risks of potential cultural and ethical discrepancies.

CHAPTER 19:
FUTURE TRENDS IN
OUTSOURCING

Outsourcing has come a long way since its inception, and it continues to evolve with time. The future of outsourcing is bright, with emerging technologies and new trends setting the pace for what lies ahead. In this chapter, we will explore the future of outsourcing and what you can expect in the years to come.

Emerging technologies and their impact on outsourcing

Emerging technologies such as artificial intelligence (AI), machine learning, the Internet of Things (IoT), and blockchain are set to revolutionize the outsourcing industry. AI and machine learning, for instance, will make it possible for outsourcing firms to automate routine tasks, freeing up their employees to focus on more complex tasks. The Internet of Things will provide outsourcing firms with real-time data, enabling them to make informed decisions and improve their services. Blockchain technology will enhance data security and privacy, making outsourcing more secure and trustworthy.

The future of outsourcing in different industries

Outsourcing will continue to play an essential role in various industries, including healthcare, finance, and manufacturing. In healthcare, outsourcing will help hospitals and clinics improve their operations, reduce costs, and enhance patient outcomes. In finance, outsourcing will enable financial institutions to streamline their operations, reduce costs, and improve their customer experience. In manufacturing, outsourcing will help companies scale their production while keeping costs under control.

New outsourcing destinations and trends

New outsourcing destinations are emerging, with countries like Vietnam, the Philippines, and Mexico becoming popular destinations for outsourcing. These countries have a highly educated workforce, a favorable business environment, and cost advantages, making them attractive to outsourcing firms. On the trend front, there has been a rise in niche outsourcing, where outsourcing firms specialize in a particular industry or function. This approach makes it possible for firms to provide highly specialized services to their clients.

The role of automation and AI in outsourcing

Automation and AI will play a critical role in the future of outsourcing. As mentioned earlier, these technologies will enable outsourcing firms to automate routine tasks, freeing up their employees to focus on more complex tasks. Additionally, AI will help outsourcing firms to improve their services, by providing insights into customer behavior and preferences. This information will help firms to provide personalized solutions to their clients, enhancing the customer experience.

The future of remote work and distributed teams

Remote work and distributed teams are becoming more popular, and this trend is set to continue in the future. Advances in technology have made it possible for teams to work together from different parts of the world seamlessly. This approach will help outsourcing firms to tap into a global talent pool, enabling them to provide high-quality services to their clients.

The challenges and opportunities of future outsourcing trends

The future of outsourcing presents both challenges and opportunities. On the one hand, new technologies and emerging trends will continue to disrupt the outsourcing industry, forcing firms to stay on top of the curve. On the other hand, these trends will provide opportunities for firms to provide high-quality services and expand their reach.

Preparing for the future of outsourcing

To stay ahead of the curve in outsourcing, you need to prepare for the future. This means staying informed about emerging technologies and trends, investing in the right technologies, and building a team that can adapt to changes. Additionally, you need to be open to new outsourcing destinations and business models, always seeking to improve the services you provide to your clients.

Staying ahead of the curve in outsourcing

To stay ahead of the curve in outsourcing, you need to continually refine your outsourcing approach and stay informed about emerging trends and best practices. Additionally, you need to build relationships with your outsourcing partners, making it possible to work together to achieve your goals.

In conclusion, the future of outsourcing is bright, with emerging technologies and new trends setting the pace for what lies ahead. To stay on top of the curve, you need to stay informed about these trends, invest in the right technologies, and build relationships with your outsourcing partners. By doing so, you will be well-positioned to take advantage of the opportunities that arise and stay ahead of the competition.

CHAPTER 20:
CONCLUSION AND
ACTION PLAN

Congratulations! You have now completed reading our book on Outsourcing Secrets and have learned a great deal about the benefits, challenges, and best practices of outsourcing. We hope that this book has provided you with the information and tools you need to make informed decisions about outsourcing for your business.

In this chapter, we will highlight some of the key takeaways from the book and provide you with an action plan to put your new knowledge into practice.

Recap of Key Takeaways

In the previous chapters, we covered various aspects of outsourcing including its definition, history, types, advantages, disadvantages, misconceptions, and factors to consider before outsourcing. We have also discussed how to find the right outsourcing partner, evaluate them, create a mutually beneficial relationship, and manage that relationship effectively. Additionally, we have talked about the pros and cons of offshore outsourcing, the cost of outsourcing, recruiting and managing a remote team, outsourcing for small businesses and startups, legal, human resources, IT, healthcare, accounting and finance, marketing and advertising, customer support, and government agencies. We have also covered cultural and ethical considerations and future trends in outsourcing.

Creating an Outsourcing Action Plan

Now it's time to put this knowledge into action and create an outsourcing action plan for your business. Here are the steps to follow:

- ❖   Review your current outsourcing strategies: Start by reviewing your current outsourcing initiatives and evaluating their effectiveness. Identify the areas of improvement and areas where outsourcing could be beneficial.

- ❖ Identify your outsourcing needs: Determine which tasks or functions should be outsourced, taking into account the cost, time, and quality considerations.

- ❖ Choose the right outsourcing partner: Conduct thorough research, evaluate potential outsourcing partners, and create a mutually beneficial relationship.

- ❖   Set clear expectations and goals: Define the roles and responsibilities, establish lines of communication, and manage cultural and ethical risks.

- ❖ Negotiate pricing and contracts: Mitigate financial risks, identify cost-saving opportunities, negotiate pricing and contracts.

- ❖ Manage outsourcing relationships effectively: Monitor performance and quality, address issues and concerns, build a long-term relationship, and measure the ROI of outsourcing.

- ❖   Continuously refine your outsourcing strategy: Stay informed about the latest outsourcing trends and best practices and update your outsourcing strategy to ensure long-term success.

Conclusion

Outsourcing can be a powerful tool for businesses to achieve their goals, increase efficiency, and reduce costs. However, it is important to approach outsourcing with caution, careful planning, and by following best practices. This book has provided you with a comprehensive guide to outsourcing and equip you with the knowledge and skills needed to make informed outsourcing decisions for your business. By following our action plan, you can create an outsourcing strategy that works for you, your business, and your goals. Remember, outsourcing is not a one size fits all solution, and the right strategy depends on your unique needs and circumstances. Be flexible, adaptable, and continuously refine your strategy to ensure long-term success.

Final Thoughts

I hope this book has provided you with valuable insights and strategies for outsourcing effectively. Outsourcing can be a powerful tool for any business, allowing you to delegate tasks and focus on what truly matters - growing your company.

Remember, outsourcing is not a one-size-fits-all solution. It requires careful consideration of your specific needs and goals. Take the time to research potential outsourcing partners and thoroughly vet them before making any decisions.

Additionally, communication is key when working with remote teams. Set expectations upfront, establish clear communication channels, and provide regular feedback to ensure everyone is on the same page.

Finally, don't be afraid to start small with outsourcing. Begin by delegating smaller tasks or projects before committing to larger ones. This will allow you to test the waters and identify any potential challenges or roadblocks before fully diving in.

As technology continues to advance and global connectivity becomes more accessible, outsourcing will only continue to grow in popularity. By mastering these outsourcing secrets, you'll be well-equipped to take advantage of this trend and stay ahead of the competition.

ABOUT THE AUTHOR

Ray Goodwin

Ray Goodwin, is the author behind this series of captivating books on Business Development and self improvement, and has left an indelible mark on the field. He was born and raised in the bustling city of London, where he developed a strong work ethic and an insatiable curiosity about the inner workings of successful businesses. Throughout his illustrious career, Ray leveraged his extensive knowledge and experience to help numerous companies flourish and prosper.

His keen insights and innovative strategies has earned him recognition, driving him to share his expertise with others. Ray believes in the power of sharing knowledge to elevate businesses and empower aspiring entrepreneurs.

Ray's dedication to his craft is evident in the numerous books he has authored on business development and self improvement. His writing style seamlessly blends practical advice, thought-provoking concepts, and real-life case studies, making his books invaluable resources for business professionals and novices alike. His ability to distill complex concepts into accessible language has greatly impacted the lives and careers of countless individuals.

Now retired from the corporate world, Ray and his beloved wife have settled in the idyllic English countryside. Surrounded by the beauty of nature, Ray finds inspiration for his writing and indulges in his hobbies.

Ray Goodwin's books continue to serve as enduring guides for those seeking success in the business world. With a wealth of experience and a deep understanding of the inner workings of businesses, Ray's work remains a testament to his passion for sharing knowledge and helping others flourish.

www.ingramcontent.com/pod-product-compliance
Lightning Source LLC
Chambersburg PA
CBHW060532010626
45794CB00022B/2110